CLASSIC RECIPES

Appetizers & soups

simple and delicious food

Wendy Hobson

ARCTURUS

ARCTURUS

This edition published in 2013 by Arcturus Publishing Limited
26/27 Bickels Yard, 151–153 Bermondsey Street,
London SE1 3HA

Design copyright ©2013 Arcturus Publishing Limited

ISBN: 978-1-78212-014-8
AD002584US

Printed in China

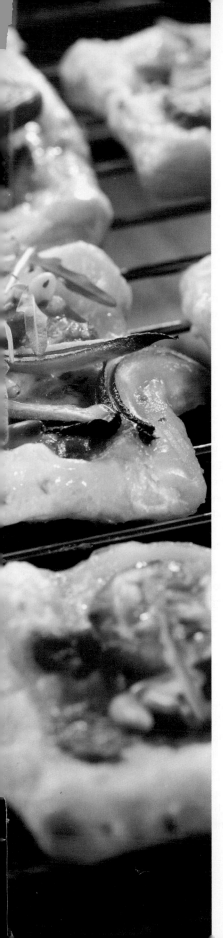

Contents

Introduction

The appetizer is many people's favorite part of the meal because so much thought goes into choosing and presenting the right combination of ingredients, in the right quantities, to set the meal off to a great start. That means applying imagination, and when you mix that with appetite, you are bound to get great food.

Appetizers are designed to whet the appetite for the meal to come, so quantities should be half that of a main course, or less. You want to take the edge off your guests' hunger but not fill them up. A well-chosen appetizer leaves you just wanting a little more, so try to avoid piling plates too high, and don't offer second helpings. If your food is good, your guests will want to eat more than they should!

Enjoying food is not just about flavor, though—it's about presentation too: the look of a dish, its colors and textures. The recipes in this book will offer you a range of opportunities to serve anything from a vibrant tomato soup to a subtle pasta dish, while the photographs will give you ideas on how to garnish and serve the dish to make it look its best. Pay particular attention to color: a white dish will show off most foods to best advantage (unless the food is also white, of course). Patterns are, more often than not, distracting and take the focus away from the food. When you serve up your first dish, your guests' eyes should go straight to the delight in store for them.

There's plenty of choice here to allow you to serve a dish that complements the main course. If you have chosen a pasta dish as your main course, then a grilled dish or a salad would offer a nice counterpoint to the meal to come; or a hearty soup could precede a roast dish. Think about color, texture, cooking method, and balance when you pair dishes together and you will get the most complementary combinations.

One great aspect of modern cooking is that we try dishes from all over the world, so we have plenty of scope for variety and choice. Here you'll find classic soups from France, hearty soups from rural Italy and light broths from Asia, as well as some real American favorites. All of them bring their own unique flavors, ingredients and styles into your kitchen. Appetizers bring together ideas from as far afield as Australia and as close to home as Mexico, allowing us to enjoy the tastes of the globe in our own kitchens.

This collection of recipes is also designed to be versatile, so you can serve the dishes however you wish to suit your lifestyle and the time you have available. Simply add a side salad and some crusty bread to a soup and you have a perfect lunch or supper dish. Make a little more pasta or a few extra kebabs for a great main course. Pile the salad ingredients in a container in the cool-bag and head off on a picnic. There are no constraints on when and how you should serve these tasty recipes. Simply add imagination and enjoy them whenever it suits you!

All the ingredients for the recipes are readily available in your local stores—there are no hard-to-come-by or obscure ingredients. In fact, many may be storecupboard staples—things you keep in your kitchen all the time. And if you don't have just the right thing, do feel free to improvise. Cooking is not a science; it should be flexible and fun.

Each recipe has a full-color photograph so that you can see what kind of dish to expect. Even beginners should find that the methods are easy to follow, as they are all laid out step-by-step, with clear instructions at every stage.

Just collect your ingredients, wash and prepare them, then work through the methods one step at a time to make some lovely dishes for your family and friends.

Italian salad

Sunshine on a plate, this dish originated in the hills of northern Italy, but can be replicated wherever you are if you choose fresh, crisp ingredients with ripe, red tomatoes full of juicy flavor. It makes its own dressing so needs nothing else.

Serves 4

4–5 slices of stale sourdough or other bread

Salt and freshly ground black pepper

100ml/3½fl oz/scant ½ cup olive oil

2 tbsp white wine vinegar

1 red onion, thinly sliced

1 red bell pepper, sliced

1 cucumber, cut into chunks

100g/4oz/1 cup black olives, pitted and sliced

8 cherry tomatoes, halved

3 garlic cloves, chopped

1. Tear the bread roughly into pieces about the size of croûtons and put them in a bowl. Season with salt and pepper and drizzle with the olive oil, then sprinkle with half the wine vinegar. Leave to stand while you prepare the salad ingredients.

2. Add the onion, pepper, cucumber, olives, tomatoes, and garlic to the bread and sprinkle with the remaining wine vinegar. Season with salt and pepper, if liked.

3. Toss the salad ingredients together gently using your hands, then serve.

Serves 4

1 peach, skinned, pitted, and diced

1 mango, peeled, pitted, and diced

3 tomatoes, diced

1 onion, finely chopped

1 yellow bell pepper, diced

1 garlic clove, finely chopped

½ small jalapeño pepper, seeded and diced

1 tbsp superfine sugar

A large cilantro sprig, chopped

1 tbsp lime juice

Salt and freshly ground black pepper

To serve

A few cilantro sprigs

Chipotle chips

Tomato and mango dip with chipotle chips

This tasty dip is lovely and chunky—the ideal starter for a spicy or robust meal, as its sweet and fruity flavor sets the taste buds tingling. To add a bit more bite, increase the amount of jalapeño pepper.

1. Mix together the peach, mango, and tomatoes, making sure you catch all the juices in the bowl.
2. Add the tomatoes, onion, pepper, garlic, and jalapeño pepper and stir together well.
3. Whisk the sugar and cilantro into the lime juice and season with salt and pepper.
4. Pour over the salsa and stir together. Garnish with cilantro and serve with chipotle chips.

Spinach filo parcels

Filo pastry is a great freezer standby. You can use it for all kinds of things, sweet and savory, including these fun little parcels. If you prefer, you can brush them with oil and bake them in a hot oven instead of deep-frying them.

Serves 4

2 scallions, finely chopped

100g/4oz/⅔ cup frozen spinach, thawed and squeezed dry

100g/4oz/½ cup cream cheese

50g/2oz/½ cup freshly grated Parmesan cheese

Salt and freshly ground black pepper

About 6 sheets filo pastry

50g/2oz/¼ cup butter, melted

Oil for deep-frying

Shredded lettuce

1. Mix together the scallions, spinach, cream cheese, and Parmesan, and season with salt and pepper.
2. Spread out a filo sheet and brush with melted butter. Place another on top, brush that with butter and place a third on top of that. Repeat separately with the other 3 sheets. Cut them into about 10cm/4in squares.
3. Heat a pan of oil for deep-frying.
4. Put a spoonful of the filling on each square, brush the edges with butter and twist the tops to make little parcels.
5. Lower a few at a time into the hot oil and fry for a minute or so until golden, then lift out of the oil using a slotted spoon, and drain on paper towels. Keep the parcels warm while you fry the remainder.
6. Serve on a bed of lettuce leaves.

Seafood and orange salad

Serves 4

450g/1lb mixed seafood, such as scallops, squid, shrimp, and salmon pieces

1 orange

4 handfuls of mixed salad leaves

1 tbsp olive oil

30g/1oz/2 tbsp all-purpose flour

Freshly ground black pepper

2 tbsp red lumpfish roe

This is a substantial starter, or it would make a lovely light lunch. You could select your seafood pieces individually at the fishmonger, or buy a pack of mixed seafood. Presentation is important for this kind of dish, so arrange your ingredients beautifully.

1. Lay out your seafood selection in order of the time it will take to cook. A small salmon steak will take about 4 minutes on each side, raw jumbo shrimp or squid 2–3 minutes, scallops about 2 minutes.
2. Peel the orange carefully, removing all the pith, then cut each segment out of its membrane. Arrange on serving plates with the salad leaves.
3. Heat a large griddle pan or skillet and drizzle it with the olive oil.

4. Toss the seafood quickly in the flour and season with a little pepper. Add to the pan in order of the length of time it will take to cook, so salmon pieces first. Sauté quickly in the pan over a medium-high heat so the seafood is just cooked through and golden on the outside but not overcooked.
5. Arrange on the plates and serve at once.

If you can use fresh pasta for this recipe, it will be particularly quick and especially delicious, but it works well with ordinary dried pasta too. A small portion makes a perfect starter, or serve this as a main course for two people.

Zucchini pasta with lemon

Serves 4

200g/7oz fresh pappardelle pasta
100g/4oz small asparagus spears
Salt and freshly ground black pepper
30g/1oz/2 tbsp butter
2 tsp olive oil
1 garlic clove, crushed
½ red bell pepper, finely diced
1 zucchini, thinly sliced
100ml/3½fl oz/scant ½ cup heavy cream
1 tbsp chopped flatleaf parsley
Finely pared zest of ½ lemon

1. Bring a large pan of lightly salted water to the boil. Add the pappardelle and asparagus and cook for 3 minutes until the pasta is *al dente*. If you are using dried pasta, add it to the pan first and cook for 5 minutes, then add the asparagus and cook for a further 3 minutes. Drain.

2. Return the empty pan to a medium heat and add the butter, oil, garlic, and pepper. Cook for 5 minutes. When it is hot and bubbling, lightly toss the zucchini slices and cook for 2 minutes.

3. Return the drained pasta and asparagus to the pan and add the cream, parsley, and lemon zest. Season with pepper.

4. Toss everything together for a few minutes until thoroughly hot and well coated in the flavored cream, then serve at once.

Liver pâté

A terrine or pâté takes a little while to prepare but is so satisfying. Your guests will be very impressed when you tell them you have made it yourself. This is a medium-textured pâté, but you can make it more coarsely or more finely textured if you prefer.

Serves 4

300ml/1pt/2½ cups milk
1 onion, halved
1 bay leaf
2 garlic cloves
450g/1lb pig's liver, trimmed
175g/6oz back bacon, rinded and trimmed
6 anchovy fillets
1 egg, lightly beaten
A pinch of freshly grated nutmeg
A pinch of ground cloves
A few thyme sprigs
Salt and freshly ground black pepper
30g/1oz/2 tbsp unsalted butter
30g/1oz/2 tbsp all-purpose flour

To serve

Crusty bread, toast or melba toast
A little butter (optional)

1. Heat the oven to 160°C/325°F/Gas 3 and grease and line a 900g/2lb loaf pan or individual ovenproof dishes.
2. Bring the milk slowly to the boil with the onion, bay leaf, and garlic. Leave to stand for 15 minutes while you prepare the ingredients.
3. Put the liver, bacon, and anchovies in a food processor and process until finely ground and well blended. Blend in the egg, nutmeg, cloves, and the leaves from 1–2 thyme sprigs. Season generously with salt and pepper.
4. Melt the butter in a pan, stir in the flour and cook for 1 minute, stirring continuously. Strain the milk and discard the onion and flavorings. Pour the milk into the pan and bring to the boil, whisking continuously until you have a smooth and creamy sauce.
5. Remove from the heat and stir in the meat mixture until well combined.
6. Spoon the mixture into the prepared loaf tin or dishes and smooth the top. Cover with greased waxed paper and place in a roasting pan filled with cold water to come a quarter of the way up the sides of the baking pan or dish. Bake in the oven for 2 hours for a loaf pan or about 1 hour for individual dishes, depending on size, until a skewer inserted in the center comes out clean. Top up with water as necessary.
7. Remove the cooking pan from the larger roasting pan and cover with a fresh piece of buttered paper. Place a heavy weight on top, such as a full can of tomatoes, and leave until cold, then transfer to the fridge, preferably overnight, still with the weight on top.
8. Either serve your individual pots or, if you have made one pâté, turn it out onto a plate and serve for guests to help themselves. Alternatively, press into individual serving dishes and garnish with a thyme sprig. Serve bread, toast or melba toast to accompany, with butter for spreading if wished.

Chicken and tomato quesadillas

Tuck into these layered tortillas, filled with chicken and tomato and lightly fried to a golden finish. You can include all kinds of fillings in this type of dish, from chunks of pumpkin to roasted zucchini and eggplant.

Serves 4

100g/4oz cooked chicken, cut into chunks
200g/7oz/1 small can of chopped tomatoes
200g/7oz/1 small can of corn
3 scallions, chopped
50g/2oz/¼ cup butter
4 corn or flour tortillas
Salt and freshly ground black pepper
1 tbsp chopped parsley

1. Put the chicken, tomatoes, corn, and scallions in a small pan, bring to a simmer and stir to heat through.
2. Meanwhile, heat a lump of the butter in a skillet and add a tortilla. Spoon one-quarter of the filling on top, fold in half and heat for a couple of minutes until golden.
3. Remove the tortilla from the pan and keep it warm. Heat and fill the remaining tortilla in the same way.
4. Sprinkle with the parsley and serve hot.

Bacon-wrapped shrimp

Serves 4

450g/1lb jumbo shrimp
225g/8oz bacon slices
About 120ml/¼pt/½ cup olive oil
½ baguette, sliced
Freshly ground black pepper
A few flatleaf parsley sprigs

This is a lovely starter to make under the broiler, in a griddle pan or on the barbecue. The only difficulty will be wanting to eat too many of these delicious mouthfuls. Buy fairly large shrimp, but not too big—one or two bites is perfect.

1. Shell the shrimp, if necessary, leaving the tail on and removing the intestinal tract—the black line down the back. Cut the bacon into long strips.
2. Wrap the bacon round the shrimp, securing with toothpicks if necessary.
3. Put the shrimp under the broiler, on the barbecue or in a hot griddle pan until they are cooked through and the bacon is beginning to crisp. If you have used raw shrimp, make sure they have turned pink right through to the center.
4. Meanwhile, heat the olive oil in a large skillet until it is fairly hot but not smoking. Carefully add the baguette slices and sauté for 1–2 minutes each side until golden and crisp. Remove from the pan and drain on paper towels.
5. Place the shrimp on top of the fried bread, season with pepper, and serve garnished with parsley.

Serves 4

1 sheet frozen puff pastry,
about 25 x 40cm/10 x 16in, or
300g/11oz puff pastry

A little flour, for dusting

1 garlic clove, finely crushed

120ml/¼pt/⅔ cup olive oil

225g/8oz cherry tomatoes

1 red onion, thinly sliced

50g/2oz/½ cup freshly grated
Parmesan cheese

Salt and freshly ground black pepper

A handful of mixed small salad leaves

Red onion and vegetable puffs

These light little pastry puffs make great starters or are equally good as nibbles to serve with drinks. It is a good idea to keep some frozen pastry in the freezer, then you can magic up a meal or a snack at a moment's notice.

1. Heat the oven to 220°C/425°F/Gas 7 and grease a cookie sheet.
2. Spread or roll out the puff pastry quite thinly on a lightly floured surface and cut into about 5cm/2in squares.
3. Whisk the garlic into the oil, then brush over the squares. Halve enough cherry tomatoes to put one on each square, reserving any left over for garnish. Spread the onion over the top and sprinkle with the grated Parmesan. Season with salt and plenty of pepper.
4. Bake in the oven for about 10–15 minutes until the pastry is puffed and golden and the cheese has melted.
5. Serve garnished with the salad leaves and any remaining tomatoes.

16

Mini burgers

Serves 4–6

For the burgers

200g/7oz ground beef

2 scallions, chopped

1 small slice of bread, made into crumbs

A pinch of dried oregano

1 egg yolk

Salt and freshly ground black pepper

For the buns

3 bacon slices, halved

6 tiny bread buns, halved

A handful of chopped lettuce

6 small slices of processed cheese

2 tomatoes, sliced

These are great fun to serve as party nibbles or starters. Find the smallest bread buns you can—or make your own—and put them together beautifully so they look just like their larger cousins. Don't make too many, though, as they are quite filling.

1. Mix together all the burger ingredients and season with salt and pepper. Press into mini burger shapes.

2. Sauté or broil the burgers for about 10 minutes, turning once or twice, until cooked through and browned on the outside.

3. Add the bacon to the pan for the last 8 minutes or so and fry until crisp.

4. Assemble the burgers by placing the burger bases on a serving plate. Cover with lettuce, then the burgers, a slice of cheese, the bacon and tomatoes. Season with salt and pepper and secure the top of the bun with a toothpick.

Stuffed crispy mushrooms

Stuffed mushrooms make quite a substantial starter, and one or two large mushroom caps is enough for most people. Other fillings you could try are chopped bacon and potato, chopped spinach with cream cheese or chopped mixed seafood with herbs.

Serves 4–6

6 large mushrooms
2 tbsp oil
120ml/¼pt/⅔ cup stock
Salt and freshly ground black pepper
3 tomatoes, chopped
1 tbsp chopped parsley
1 tsp chopped thyme
60ml/2fl oz/4 tbsp heavy cream
200g/7oz/1 cup grated Swiss cheese

To garnish
A few lettuce leaves
A few herb sprigs
A spoonful of sour cream

1. Heat the oven to 200°C/400°F/Gas 6 and lightly grease a baking pan.
2. Take the stems off the mushrooms. Place the mushroom caps, gill-sides up, in the baking pan. Drizzle with the oil and spoon the stock over, then season with salt and pepper. Pop them in the oven for 15 minutes while you make the filling.
3. Chop the mushroom stems and put them in a bowl with the tomatoes, parsley, thyme, and cream. Season with salt and pepper.
4. Remove the mushrooms from the oven and pile the filling on top. Sprinkle with the cheese, covering some completely and others just partially.
5. Return the mushrooms to the oven for a further 15–20 minutes until the cheese is melted and bubbling, then serve garnished with lettuce leaves and herb sprigs, with a spoonful of sour cream on any cheese-free mushrooms.

Rainbow kebabs

While they're perfect for the barbecue, these colorful kebabs cook just as well under the broiler so don't wait until barbecue season to try them. For maximum impact, mix the different colors as you thread the ingredients on to the skewers.

Serves 4

1 zucchini
1 red bell pepper, cut into strips
1 yellow pepper, cut into strips
1 red onion, cut into small wedges
8 cherry tomatoes
225g/8oz halloumi cheese, cut into cubes
3 tbsp olive oil
Salt and freshly ground black pepper

1. If you are using wooden skewers, put them in water to soak for 30 minutes before you cook.
2. Heat the broiler or a griddle pan.
3. Prepare the vegetables and divide them evenly between 8 skewers. Thread the ingredients on the skewers, alternating colors and textures. Brush with the oil and season with salt and pepper.
4. Broil the kebabs for about 10 minutes, turning frequently, until browned on all sides. Alternatively, cook on the barbecue or on a hot griddle pan.
5. Serve immediately while hot.

Mushroom soup

A mix of different mushrooms makes a nice change for this soup. You could also include some dried porcini mushrooms to add extra depth to the flavor—soak and drain them first. The result is a wonderfully creamy soup, with succulent chunks of mushroom.

Serves 4

30g/1oz/2 tbsp butter
225g/8oz/2 cups mushrooms, sliced
30g/1oz/2 tbsp all-purpose flour
300ml/½pt/1¼ cups vegetable or chicken stock
300ml/½pt/1¼ cups milk
1 tbsp chopped parsley
1 small rosemary sprig
1 small thyme sprig
Salt and freshly ground black pepper
1 tbsp brandy or lemon juice
3 tbsp cream

1. Melt the butter in a large pan and sauté the mushrooms for a few minutes until the juices start to run.
2. Sprinkle in the flour and cook for 2 minutes, stirring continuously.
3. Pour in the stock and milk and whisk until the soup comes to a simmer and is smooth.
4. Add the parsley, rosemary, and thyme, and season with salt and pepper. Simmer gently for 10 minutes.
5. Remove the herb sprigs, stir in the brandy or lemon juice, then the cream, and heat gently until you are ready to serve. Do not allow the soup to boil.

French onion soup

The intense flavor of this soup is created by the long, slow cooking of the onions to caramelize them and turn them to a wonderfully sweet, soft brown. A slice of cheese-topped bread is then floated in the soup.

Serves 4

50g/2oz/¼ cup butter
2 tbsp oil
450g/1lb onions, sliced
1 garlic clove, chopped
1 tsp brown sugar
1 tbsp cornstarch
1.5 litres/2½pt/6 cups beef stock
Salt and freshly ground black pepper
4 thick slices of French bread
100g/4oz/1 cup grated Gruyère cheese
1 tbsp chopped parsley

1. Heat half the butter and the oil in a large pan and sauté the onions and garlic over a low heat, stirring, until they begin to soften. Cover and cook for a further 15 minutes.
2. Remove the lid, sprinkle with the sugar and continue to cook over a low heat until the onions are very soft, browned and beginning to caramelize. This may take 20 minutes but it cannot be rushed by turning up the heat as this will simply burn the onions. Stir occasionally.
3. Put the cornstarch in a ramekin or small bowl and add 2 tbsp of the stock. Add the remainder to the pan and bring to a simmer. Cover and simmer over the lowest possible heat for about 1 hour, stirring occasionally.
4. Heat the broiler.
5. Blend the cornstarch smoothly with the stock and add it to the pan, whisking continuously until the soup is thick and smooth. Season with salt and pepper.
6. Toast one side of the bread. Spread the untoasted side with the remaining butter, sprinkle with the cheese and broil for a few minutes until golden and bubbling.
7. Float the bread in the soup and sprinkle with parsley to serve.

Everyone's favorite Chinese soup, this is easy to make but looks very impressive. If you have some leftover cooked chicken, simply fry the garlic and ginger at Step 1 with a little less oil, then add the shredded cooked chicken with the stock and corn.

Chinese chicken and corn soup

Serves 4

2 tsp oil
1 chicken breast, cut into thin strips
1 garlic clove, finely chopped
1.5cm/¾in piece of ginger root, peeled and finely chopped
A dash of sesame oil
600ml/1pt/2½ cups chicken stock
250g/8 oz/1 small can of creamed corn
2 tsp cornstarch
1 tsp water
1 egg, lightly beaten
1 tbsp light soy sauce (optional)
Salt and freshly ground black pepper
30g/1oz/2 tbsp frozen corn kernels

1. Heat the oil in a large pan and sauté the chicken with the garlic, ginger, and sesame oil over a low heat until just cooked but not browned.
2. Add the stock and corn and bring to the boil. Simmer for 10 minutes.
3. Shred the chicken finely and return to the pan.
4. Blend the cornstarch and water to a paste, then beat it into the soup, stirring until thickened. Simmer for 5 minutes.
5. Put the beaten egg into a small jug. Keep whisking the soup while you pour in the beaten egg so that it distributes in strands through the soup.
6. Whisk in the soy sauce, if liked, and season to taste with salt and pepper before serving garnished with the corn kernels.

Bouillabaisse

This classic soup hails from Marseilles in southern France, where the freshest fish is used, straight from the fishing vessels. Use a wide variety if you can—ideally at least three of fish and three of shellfish, although it will taste good with fewer!

Serves 4

For the soup

2 tbsp olive oil

1 onion, sliced

2 garlic cloves, chopped

1 fennel bulb, diced

200g/7oz/1 small can tomatoes

1 tbsp tomato paste

A pinch of saffron strands

150ml/¼pt/⅔ cup dry white wine

1 bay leaf

1 thyme sprig

1 parsley sprig

1 marjoram sprig

2 litres/3½pt/8½ cups water or fish stock

300g/12oz mixed seafood, such as prawns, mussels, clams, scrubbed

450g/1lb fish fillets, such as sea bream, mullet, pollack

Salt and freshly ground black pepper

For the rouille

3 garlic cloves, crushed

A pinch of saffron strands

1 egg yolk

½ tsp French mustard

200ml/7fl oz/scant 1 cup olive oil

½ tsp cayenne pepper

Juice of 1 lemon

1. Heat the oil in a large pan and sauté the onion, garlic and fennel over a low heat, stirring, until just softened.
2. Stir in the tomatoes, tomato paste, and saffron, then add the wine, bring to a simmer, and add the bay leaf and herb sprigs. Pour in the water or stock, bring to the boil, and simmer for about 5 minutes.
3. Add the seafood and simmer for 2 minutes, discarding any shells that do not open. Add the fish and simmer for 5 minutes until all the fish is cooked. Season with salt and pepper.
4. Meanwhile, make the rouille. Crush the garlic to a paste with the saffron, then work in the egg yolk and mustard.
5. Gradually add the olive oil in a steady stream, whisking all the time, so that the oil is incorporated into the sauce, as though you were making mayonnaise. Whisk in the lemon juice and season with salt and pepper.
6. Stir the rouille into the soup and serve.

Thai-style spicy shrimp soup

Asian soups often have a thin broth with plenty of whole fish or vegetables. This is quite a spicy soup, so if you prefer your appetizers with a little less bite, just hold back on the chilis a little. You can also make it with cooked chicken.

Serves 4

900ml/1½pt/3¾ cups fish stock

2 lemongrass stalks, chopped

3 kaffir lime leaves

4 small red chilis, deseeded and finely chopped

5cm/2in piece of galangal or ginger root, chopped

2 tbsp fish sauce (*tam pla*)

1 tbsp Thai chili paste

4 tbsp lime juice

50g/2oz/½ cup straw mushrooms, sliced

20 raw shelled shrimp

1 cilantro sprig

1. Put the stock in a large pan and bring to a simmer.
2. Add the lemongrass, lime leaves, chilis, and galangal, return to the boil, then simmer for 3 minutes.
3. Add the fish sauce, chili paste, lime juice, and mushrooms, and return to a simmer for about 5 minutes until the mushrooms begin to soften.
4. Add the shrimp and simmer for a few minutes until cooked through, when they will turn pink.
5. Serve garnished with cilantro.

Corn and potato chowder

A favorite from New England, this soup should be cooked long and slow so you can serve your guests generous portions of the most flavorsome, thick and creamy soup, with the colorful corn, herb, and tomato garnish in superb contrast.

Serves 4

3 bacon slices, rinded and finely chopped

1 tbsp oil (optional)

1 onion, chopped

2 potatoes, peeled and diced

300ml/½pt/1¼ cups boiling water or stock

200g/7oz/1 small can of corn, drained

200g/7oz/1 small can of creamed corn, drained

200g/7oz/1 small can of evaporated milk

150ml/¼pt/½ cup milk

Salt and freshly ground black pepper

1 tbsp chopped parsley

A pinch of cayenne pepper

1. Heat a large pan and sauté the bacon in its own fat until crisp. Remove from the pan and set aside.

2. Add the oil, if necessary, and the onions and cook over a medium-low heat until soft but not browned.

3. Add the potatoes and water or stock and bring to the boil. Cover and simmer for 10 minutes.

4. Reserve 2 tbsp of the whole corn kernels for garnish and add the remainder to the pan with the creamed corn. Stir until hot.

5. Add the evaporated milk and the milk, bring to a simmer, and season with salt and pepper. Simmer over the lowest possible heat for about 20 minutes, stirring regularly, without allowing the soup to boil. Add a little water if the soup needs to be thinner, or heat for a little longer to thicken.

6. Season to taste with salt and pepper and serve sprinkled with the reserved corn and bacon, the parsley, and a pinch of cayenne.

Serves 4

1 tbsp olive oil

15g/½oz/1 tbsp butter

50g/2oz pancetta or bacon, rinded and chopped

1 onion, chopped

1–2 garlic cloves, chopped

1 carrot, chopped

1 celery stick, chopped

1 potato, peeled and chopped

400g/14oz/1 large can chopped tomatoes

1 tbsp tomato paste

1 litre/1¾pts/4¼ cups vegetable stock

50g/2oz small pasta

400g/14oz/1 large can small navy beans, drained and rinsed

A large handful of frozen peas

2 basil sprigs

To serve

50g/2oz/½ cup grated Parmesan cheese

Crusty bread

Minestrone

Traditionally, this 'big soup' would be made with dried beans and a variety of vegetables, depending on what was available. However, canned beans are much more convenient than dried, which need to be soaked overnight.

1. Heat the oil and butter in a large pan and sauté the bacon, onion, garlic, carrot, and celery for a few minutes over a low heat until soft but not browned.

2. Add the potato, tomatoes, and tomato paste and stir everything together until hot.

3. Add the stock, bring to a simmer, and simmer for 15 minutes.

4. Add the pasta, return to the boil, then simmer gently for about 5 minutes until the pasta is almost cooked.

5. Add the beans and peas. Reserve a few basil leaves for garnish, chop the remainder and add them to the pan. Bring to a simmer and simmer gently for about 10 minutes until everything is cooked and the soup is rich and thick.

6. Garnish with basil and Parmesan and serve with crusty bread.

One of our favorite comfort foods, there is nothing quite like a bowl of hot tomato soup to soothe away the cares of a difficult day. In this version, the addition of basil and a hint of spice make it particularly delicious.

Tomato and basil soup

Serves 4

1 tbsp oil

1 onion, chopped

1 garlic clove, chopped

1 celery stick, chopped

1 carrot, chopped

450g/1lb tomatoes, chopped, or 400g/14oz/1 large can chopped tomatoes

2 tbsp tomato paste

150ml/¼pt/⅔ cup dry white wine (optional)

2 basil sprigs

600ml/1pt/2½ cups vegetable stock or water, and more for thinning if liked

½ tsp chili powder (optional)

Salt and freshly ground black pepper

2 tbsp heavy or sour cream

1. Heat the oil in a large pan and sauté the onion, garlic, celery, and carrot for about 5 minutes over a medium-low heat until soft but not browned.
2. Add the tomatoes and tomato paste and stir together well for 2–3 minutes.
3. Add the wine, if using, bring to the boil, and boil for 1 minute.
4. Chop one of the basil sprigs and add it to the pan with the stock or water and the chili, if using. Season with salt and pepper. Bring to the boil, cover, and simmer gently for about 20 minutes until all the vegetables are tender.
5. Purée the soup in a blender or food processor or use a hand blender. If you prefer a really smooth soup, rub it through a sieve.
6. Return it to the pan, taste and season with salt and pepper, and heat through. Adjust the thickness of the soup to how you prefer it by adding a little boiling water or stock.
7. Serve garnished with basil and with a swirl of cream in each bowl.

Scotch broth

Originally, this hearty soup would have been constantly bubbling over the hearth, with extra meat or vegetables added as they were available. Often made with beef, this is a lamb-based version, nourishing enough to serve as a meal in its own right.

Serves 4

2 tbsp oil or butter
225g/8oz lamb, diced
2 litres/3½pts/8½ cups chicken or vegetable stock
Salt and freshly ground black pepper
1 onion, sliced
2 leeks, chopped
2 carrots, sliced
1 small turnip, peeled and chopped
½ rutabaga, peeled and chopped (optional)
50g/2oz/¼ cup pearl barley
2 tbsp chopped parsley

1. Heat half the oil or butter over a medium heat in a large pan. Add the meat and cook until sealed and beginning to brown.
2. Add the stock and season with salt and pepper. Bring to the boil, then cover and simmer for 1½ hours.
3. Meanwhile, heat the remaining oil in a separate pan and sauté the onion and leeks over a medium-low heat, stirring, until they are beginning to soften.
4. Add them to the meat with the carrots, turnip, rutabaga, if using, and pearl barley. Bring to a simmer, cover, and simmer gently for a further 1 hour until the meat and vegetables are tender. You may need to top up with a little more hot stock or water during cooking
5. Check the seasoning, adjusting if necessary, and serve sprinkled with the parsley.